The
UNITED
STATES
PRESIDENTS

Franklin D.
ROOSEVELT

Megan M. Gunderson

Big Buddy Books
An Imprint of Abdo Publishing
abdopublishing.com

abdopublishing.com

Published by Abdo Publishing, a division of ABDO, PO Box 398166, Minneapolis, Minnesota 55439.
Copyright © 2017 by Abdo Consulting Group, Inc. International copyrights reserved in all countries. No
part of this book may be reproduced in any form without written permission from the publisher. Big Buddy
Books™ is a trademark and logo of Abdo Publishing.

Printed in the United States of America, North Mankato, Minnesota
062016
092016

THIS BOOK CONTAINS
RECYCLED MATERIALS

Design: Sarah DeYoung, Mighty Media, Inc.
Production: Mighty Media, Inc.
Editor: Lauren Kukla
Cover Photograph: Getty Images
Interior Photographs: Alamy (pp. 7, 17, 29); AP Images (pp. 6, 11, 23, 25); Corbis (p. 5); Getty Images
     (pp. 9, 15); Library of Congress (p. 27); Photo Researchers (p. 21); Picture History (pp. 13, 19)

Cataloging-in-Publication Data

Names: Gunderson, Megan M., author.
Title: Franklin D. Roosevelt / by Megan M. Gunderson.
Description: Minneapolis, MN : Abdo Publishing, [2017] | Series: United States
     presidents | Includes bibliographical references and index.
Identifiers: LCCN 2015957490 | ISBN 9781680781151 (lib. bdg.) |
     ISBN 9781680775358 (ebook)
Subjects: LCSH: Roosevelt, Franklin D. (Franklin Delano), 1882-1945--Juvenile
     literature. | Presidents--United States--Biography--Juvenile literature. |
     United States--Politics and government--1933-1945--Juvenile literature.
Classification: DDC 973.917/092 [B]--dc23
LC record available at http://lccn.loc.gov/2015957490

Contents

Franklin Roosevelt

Franklin D. Roosevelt was the thirty-second US president. He faced many **challenges**. Roosevelt led the nation through two of the worst problems of the 1900s. They were the **Great Depression** and **World War II**.

Roosevelt was elected president four times. He served longer than any other president. He became one of the most important presidents in US history.

Timeline

1882

On January 30, Franklin Delano Roosevelt was born in Hyde Park, New York.

1921

Roosevelt became ill with **polio**.

1905

On March 17, Roosevelt married Anna Eleanor Roosevelt.

1928

Roosevelt was elected governor of New York.

1941

On December 7, Japan attacked Pearl Harbor in Hawaii. The next day, the United States entered **World War II**.

1933

On March 4, Roosevelt became the thirty-second US president.

1945

On April 12, President Franklin D. Roosevelt died.

Young Franklin

Franklin Delano Roosevelt was born on January 30, 1882, in Hyde Park, New York. His parents were named James and Sara. When Franklin was 14, he left home to go to school in Massachusetts.

★ FAST FACTS ★

Born: January 30, 1882

Wife: Anna Eleanor Roosevelt (1884–1962)

Children: six

Political Party: Democrat

Age at Inauguration: 51

Years Served: 1933–1945

Vice Presidents: John Nance Garner, Henry A. Wallace, Harry S. Truman

Died: April 12, 1945, age 63

James Roosevelt (*bottom left*) was a wealthy landowner and a railroad businessman. Sara (*bottom right*) came from a wealthy shipping family.

College Life

After finishing school, Roosevelt went to college in Cambridge, Massachusetts. There, he studied history, **economics**, and science. Then, in 1904, Roosevelt began law school in New York City, New York.

On March 17, 1905, he married Anna Eleanor Roosevelt. She went by Eleanor. President Theodore Roosevelt was her uncle.

★ DID YOU KNOW? ★

Roosevelt and Eleanor were fifth cousins.

The Roosevelts had six children, but one son died as a baby.

State Senator

Roosevelt passed the test to become a **lawyer** in 1907. He then started working for a New York law firm. However, he soon began thinking about working in **politics** instead.

Democratic Party leaders believed Roosevelt could be a successful politician. He had a well-known name. He also had enough money to run a strong campaign.

In 1910, Roosevelt ran for state senator. He won the election by more than 1,000 votes. Then, in 1912, Roosevelt was reelected.

Roosevelt worked hard as a state senator. He fought to give women the right to vote.

Leading the Navy

While serving in the state senate, Roosevelt worked for Woodrow Wilson's 1912 presidential campaign. Wilson won the election. Then, in 1913, he named Roosevelt assistant **secretary of the navy**.

In 1917, United States entered **World War I**. As secretary, Roosevelt worked hard during the war. He made the navy bigger and stronger.

By the end of the war, Roosevelt had learned much. He was known nationally. It was time to run for a higher **political** office.

As assistant secretary of the navy, Roosevelt kept the navy prepared. He also looked for ways to make it better.

New Challenges

In 1920, James M. Cox ran for president. Roosevelt became his **running mate**. Cox and Roosevelt lost the election.

Then in August 1921, Roosevelt became partly **paralyzed**. He learned he had **polio**. He would never walk again without help.

In 1924, Roosevelt went to Warm Springs, Georgia. There, he treated his paralysis in warm **mineral** water. Roosevelt decided to help other people with polio. In 1927, he formed the Georgia Warm Springs **Foundation** to accomplish this.

Roosevelt's cottage in Warm Springs became known as the "Little White House."

Governor

Despite his illness, Roosevelt kept active in **politics**. In 1928, he was elected governor of New York. He was reelected in 1930.

By 1931, Americans were suffering through the **Great Depression**. In 1932, **Democrats** chose Roosevelt to run for president. He gave a speech promising "a new deal" for Americans.

Many Americans believed Roosevelt's New Deal would help the **economy**. The presidential election took place in November 1932. Roosevelt easily beat President Herbert Hoover.

Roosevelt visited 38 states during his 1932 presidential campaign.

President

Roosevelt became president on March 4, 1933. The first three months of his first term were very busy. Many of his New Deal **programs** were created during this time.

One program was the Civilian Conservation Corps (CCC). The CCC

★ SUPREME COURT ★ APPOINTMENTS

Hugo L. Black: 1937

Stanley F. Reed: 1938

Felix Frankfurter: 1939

William O. Douglas: 1939

Frank Murphy: 1940

Harlan Fiske Stone: 1941

James F. Byrnes: 1941

Robert H. Jackson: 1941

Wiley B. Rutledge: 1943

The Franklin Delano Roosevelt Memorial is in Washington, DC. Statues there show the problems many people faced during the Great Depression.

helped take care of the nation's natural areas. It also gave jobs to young men.

In 1935, Roosevelt continued to create **programs** with the Second New Deal. The Works Progress Administration created jobs for millions of people. Workers built bridges, roads, airports, and other projects.

As time passed, the US government was becoming more powerful. Some people felt Roosevelt had too much power. As a result, several New Deal programs ended.

In 1936, Roosevelt was up for reelection. He ran against Alfred M. Landon. Roosevelt easily won.

PRESIDENT ROOSEVELT'S CABINET

First Term
March 4, 1933–January 20, 1937

- ★ **STATE:** Cordell Hull
- ★ **TREASURY:** W.H. Woodin, Henry Morgenthau Jr. (from January 8, 1934)
- ★ **WAR:** George H. Dern
- ★ **NAVY:** Claude A. Swanson
- ★ **ATTORNEY GENERAL:** Homer S. Cummings
- ★ **INTERIOR:** Harold L. Ickes
- ★ **AGRICULTURE:** Henry A. Wallace
- ★ **COMMERCE:** Daniel C. Roper
- ★ **LABOR:** Frances Perkins

Second Term
January 20, 1937–January 20, 1941

- ★ **STATE:** Cordell Hull
- ★ **TREASURY:** Henry Morgenthau Jr.
- ★ **WAR:** Harry H. Woodring, Henry L. Stimson (from July 10, 1940)
- ★ **NAVY:** Claude A. Swanson, Charles Edison (from January 11, 1940), Frank Knox (from July 10, 1940)
- ★ **ATTORNEY GENERAL:** Homer S. Cummings, Frank Murphy (from January 17, 1939), Robert H. Jackson (from January 18, 1940)
- ★ **INTERIOR:** Harold L. Ickes
- ★ **AGRICULTURE:** Henry A. Wallace, Claude R. Wickard (from September 5, 1940)
- ★ **COMMERCE:** Daniel C. Roper, Harry L. Hopkins (from January 23, 1939), Jesse H. Jones (from September 19, 1940)
- ★ **LABOR:** Frances Perkins

Third Term
January 20, 1941–January 20, 1945

- ★ **STATE:** Cordell Hull, Edward R. Stettinius (from December 1, 1944)
- ★ **TREASURY:** Henry Morgenthau Jr.
- ★ **WAR:** Henry L. Stimson
- ★ **NAVY:** Frank Knox, James Forrestal (from May 18, 1944)
- ★ **ATTORNEY GENERAL:** Robert H. Jackson, Francis Biddle (from September 5, 1941)
- ★ **INTERIOR:** Harold L. Ickes
- ★ **AGRICULTURE:** Claude R. Wickard
- ★ **COMMERCE:** Jesse H. Jones
- ★ **LABOR:** Frances Perkins

Fourth Term
January 20, 1945–April 12, 1945

- ★ **STATE:** Edward R. Stettinius
- ★ **TREASURY:** Henry Morgenthau Jr.
- ★ **WAR:** Henry L. Stimson
- ★ **NAVY:** James Forrestal
- ★ **ATTORNEY GENERAL:** Francis Biddle
- ★ **INTERIOR:** Harold L. Ickes
- ★ **AGRICULTURE:** Claude R. Wickard
- ★ **COMMERCE:** Jesse H. Jones, Henry A. Wallace (from March 2, 1945)
- ★ **LABOR:** Frances Perkins

Vice President
John Nance Garner

World War II

In 1940, Roosevelt thought about stepping down. No US president had ever served more than two terms. But that year, the **Democrats** chose Roosevelt to run for a third term. He won!

World War II had begun in 1939. Germany had taken over much of Europe. It was now planning to attack Great Britain. Roosevelt felt the United States would soon be in danger. However, many Americans did not want to join the war.

Roosevelt signed the Lend-Lease Act in 1941. It allowed the United States to help Great Britain without officially joining the war.

Then, on December 7, 1941, Japanese airplanes attacked the US naval base at Pearl Harbor, Hawaii. They sank ships and destroyed airplanes. The attack killed more than 2,000 Americans.

The next day, the United States was at war with Japan. By December 11, the United States was also at war with Germany and Italy. Roosevelt helped lead the **Allies** in their war against the **Axis Powers**.

Another election took place in 1944. Roosevelt believed he should remain president. Voters agreed. For the first time in US history, a president was elected to a fourth term.

Harry S. Truman was elected Roosevelt's vice president in 1944. He served as the thirty-third US president from 1945 to 1953.

Final Days

By January 1945, **World War II** was almost over. In February, Roosevelt met with **Allied** leaders. They discussed Europe's future.

After the meeting, Roosevelt returned to the United States. On April 12, he had a terrible headache. A few hours later, he died. Vice President Harry S. Truman became president.

Roosevelt led the country for longer than any president before or since. Not everyone agreed with his ideas. Yet Roosevelt was seen as a strong and much-loved leader.

Seated left to right: British Prime Minister Winston Churchill, Roosevelt, and Soviet Union leader Joseph Stalin in February 1945.

Office of the President

Branches of Government

The US government has three branches. They are the executive, legislative, and judicial branches. Each branch has some power over the others. This is called a system of checks and balances.

★ Executive Branch

The executive branch enforces laws. It is made up of the president, the vice president, and the president's cabinet. The president represents the United States around the world. He or she also signs bills into law and leads the military.

★ Legislative Branch

The legislative branch makes laws, maintains the military, and regulates trade. It also has the power to declare war. This branch includes the Senate and the House of Representatives. Together, these two houses form Congress.

★ Judicial Branch

The judicial branch interprets laws. It is made up of district courts, courts of appeals, and the Supreme Court. District courts try cases. Sometimes people disagree with a trial's outcome. Then he or she may appeal. If a court of appeals supports the ruling, a person may appeal to the Supreme Court.

Qualifications for Office

To be president, a candidate must be at least 35 years old. The person must be a natural-born US citizen. He or she must also have lived in the United States for at least 14 years.

Electoral College

The US presidential election is an indirect election. Voters from each state choose electors. These electors represent their state in the Electoral College. Each elector has one electoral vote. Electors cast their vote for the candidate with the highest number of votes from people in their state. A candidate must receive the majority of Electoral College votes to win.

Term of Office

Each president may be elected to two four-year terms. The presidential election is held on the Tuesday after the first Monday in November. The president is sworn in on January 20 of the following year. At that time, he or she takes the oath of office.
It states:

> I do solemnly swear (or affirm) that I will faithfully execute the office of President of the United States, and will to the best of my ability, preserve, protect and defend the Constitution of the United States.

31

Line of Succession

The Presidential Succession Act of 1947 states who becomes president if the president cannot serve. The vice president is first in the line. Next are the Speaker of the House and the President Pro Tempore of the Senate. It may happen that none of these individuals is able to serve. Then the office falls to the president's cabinet members. They would take office in the order in which each department was created:

Secretary of State

Secretary of the Treasury

Secretary of Defense

Attorney General

Secretary of the Interior

Secretary of Agriculture

Secretary of Commerce

Secretary of Labor

Secretary of Health and Human Services

Secretary of Housing
   and Urban Development

Secretary of Transportation

Secretary of Energy

Secretary of Education

Secretary of Veterans Affairs

Secretary of Homeland Security

Benefits

★ While in office, the president receives a salary. It is $400,000 per year. He or she lives in the White House. The president also has 24-hour Secret Service protection.

★ The president may travel on a Boeing 747 jet. This special jet is called Air Force One. It can hold 70 passengers. It has kitchens, a dining room, sleeping areas, and more. Air Force One can fly halfway around the world before needing to refuel. It can even refuel in flight!

★ When the president travels by car, he or she uses Cadillac One. It is a Cadillac Deville that has been modified. The car has heavy armor and communications systems. The president may even take Cadillac One along when visiting other countries.

★ The president also travels on a helicopter. It is called Marine One. It may also be taken along when the president visits other countries.

★ Sometimes the president needs to get away with family and friends. Camp David is the official presidential retreat. It is located in Maryland. The US Navy maintains the retreat. The US Marine Corps keeps it secure. The camp offers swimming, tennis, golf, and hiking.

★ When the president leaves office, he or she receives lifetime Secret Service protection. He or she also receives a yearly pension of $203,700. The former president also receives money for office space, supplies, and staff.

PRESIDENTS AND THEIR TERMS

PRESIDENT	PARTY	TOOK OFFICE	LEFT OFFICE	TERMS SERVED	VICE PRESIDENT
George Washington	None	April 30, 1789	March 4, 1797	Two	John Adams
John Adams	Federalist	March 4, 1797	March 4, 1801	One	Thomas Jefferson
Thomas Jefferson	Democratic-Republican	March 4, 1801	March 4, 1809	Two	Aaron Burr, George Clinton
James Madison	Democratic-Republican	March 4, 1809	March 4, 1817	Two	George Clinton, Elbridge Gerry
James Monroe	Democratic-Republican	March 4, 1817	March 4, 1825	Two	Daniel D. Tompkins
John Quincy Adams	Democratic-Republican	March 4, 1825	March 4, 1829	One	John C. Calhoun
Andrew Jackson	Democrat	March 4, 1829	March 4, 1837	Two	John C. Calhoun, Martin Van Buren
Martin Van Buren	Democrat	March 4, 1837	March 4, 1841	One	Richard M. Johnson
William H. Harrison	Whig	March 4, 1841	April 4, 1841	Died During First Term	John Tyler
John Tyler	Whig	April 6, 1841	March 4, 1845	Completed Harrison's Term	Office Vacant
James K. Polk	Democrat	March 4, 1845	March 4, 1849	One	George M. Dallas
Zachary Taylor	Whig	March 5, 1849	July 9, 1850	Died During First Term	Millard Fillmore

PRESIDENT	PARTY	TOOK OFFICE	LEFT OFFICE	TERMS SERVED	VICE PRESIDENT
Millard Fillmore	Whig	July 10, 1850	March 4, 1853	Completed Taylor's Term	Office Vacant
Franklin Pierce	Democrat	March 4, 1853	March 4, 1857	One	William R.D. King
James Buchanan	Democrat	March 4, 1857	March 4, 1861	One	John C. Breckinridge
Abraham Lincoln	Republican	March 4, 1861	April 15, 1865	Served One Term, Died During Second Term	Hannibal Hamlin, Andrew Johnson
Andrew Johnson	Democrat	April 15, 1865	March 4, 1869	Completed Lincoln's Second Term	Office Vacant
Ulysses S. Grant	Republican	March 4, 1869	March 4, 1877	Two	Schuyler Colfax, Henry Wilson
Rutherford B. Hayes	Republican	March 3, 1877	March 4, 1881	One	William A. Wheeler
James A. Garfield	Republican	March 4, 1881	September 19, 1881	Died During First Term	Chester Arthur
Chester Arthur	Republican	September 20, 1881	March 4, 1885	Completed Garfield's Term	Office Vacant
Grover Cleveland	Democrat	March 4, 1885	March 4, 1889	One	Thomas A. Hendricks
Benjamin Harrison	Republican	March 4, 1889	March 4, 1893	One	Levi P. Morton
Grover Cleveland	Democrat	March 4, 1893	March 4, 1897	One	Adlai E. Stevenson
William McKinley	Republican	March 4, 1897	September 14, 1901	Served One Term, Died During Second Term	Garret A. Hobart, Theodore Roosevelt

PRESIDENT	PARTY	TOOK OFFICE	LEFT OFFICE	TERMS SERVED	VICE PRESIDENT
Theodore Roosevelt	Republican	September 14, 1901	March 4, 1909	Completed McKinley's Second Term, Served One Term	Office Vacant, Charles Fairbanks
William Taft	Republican	March 4, 1909	March 4, 1913	One	James S. Sherman
Woodrow Wilson	Democrat	March 4, 1913	March 4, 1921	Two	Thomas R. Marshall
Warren G. Harding	Republican	March 4, 1921	August 2, 1923	Died During First Term	Calvin Coolidge
Calvin Coolidge	Republican	August 3, 1923	March 4, 1929	Completed Harding's Term, Served One Term	Office Vacant, Charles Dawes
Herbert Hoover	Republican	March 4, 1929	March 4, 1933	One	Charles Curtis
Franklin D. Roosevelt	Democrat	March 4, 1933	April 12, 1945	Served Three Terms, Died During Fourth Term	John Nance Garner, Henry A. Wallace, Harry S. Truman
Harry S. Truman	Democrat	April 12, 1945	January 20, 1953	Completed Roosevelt's Fourth Term, Served One Term	Office Vacant, Alben Barkley
Dwight D. Eisenhower	Republican	January 20, 1953	January 20, 1961	Two	Richard Nixon
John F. Kennedy	Democrat	January 20, 1961	November 22, 1963	Died During First Term	Lyndon B. Johnson
Lyndon B. Johnson	Democrat	November 22, 1963	January 20, 1969	Completed Kennedy's Term, Served One Term	Office Vacant, Hubert H. Humphrey
Richard Nixon	Republican	January 20, 1969	August 9, 1974	Completed First Term, Resigned During Second Term	Spiro T. Agnew, Gerald Ford

PRESIDENT	PARTY	TOOK OFFICE	LEFT OFFICE	TERMS SERVED	VICE PRESIDENT
Gerald Ford	Republican	August 9, 1974	January 20, 1977	Completed Nixon's Second Term	Nelson A. Rockefeller
Jimmy Carter	Democrat	January 20, 1977	January 20, 1981	One	Walter Mondale
Ronald Reagan	Republican	January 20, 1981	January 20, 1989	Two	George H.W. Bush
George H.W. Bush	Republican	January 20, 1989	January 20, 1993	One	Dan Quayle
Bill Clinton	Democrat	January 20, 1993	January 20, 2001	Two	Al Gore
George W. Bush	Republican	January 20, 2001	January 20, 2009	Two	Dick Cheney
Barack Obama	Democrat	January 20, 2009	January 20, 2017	Two	Joe Biden

"The love of freedom is still fierce and steady in the nation today."

Franklin D. Roosevelt

★ WRITE TO THE PRESIDENT ★

You may write to the president at:
The White House
1600 Pennsylvania Avenue NW
Washington, DC 20500

You may e-mail the president at:
comments@whitehouse.gov

Glossary

allies—people, groups, or nations working together. During World War II, Great Britain, France, the United States, and the Soviet Union were called the Allies.

Axis Powers—countries that fought against the Allies in World War II. Germany, Italy, and Japan were called the Axis Powers.

challenge (CHA-luhnj)—something that tests one's strengths or abilities.

Democratic—relating to the Democratic political party. Democrats believe in social change and strong government.

economy—the way that a country produces, sells, and buys goods and services. The study of producing, buying, and selling is called economics.

foundation (faun-DAY-shuhn)—an organization that controls gifts of money and services.

Great Depression—the period from 1929 to 1942 of worldwide economic trouble. There was little buying and selling, and many people could not find work.

lawyer (LAW-yuhr)—a person who gives people advice on laws or represents them in court.

mineral—a natural substance that makes up rocks and other parts of nature.

paralyzed (PEHR-uh-lized)—affected with a loss of feeling or motion in part of the body. This condition is called paralysis.

polio—the common name for poliomyelitis, a disease that sometimes leaves people paralyzed.

politics—the art or science of government. Something referring to politics is political. A person who is active in politics is a politician.

program—a plan for doing something.

running mate—someone running for vice president with another person running for president in an election.

secretary of the navy—a member of the president's cabinet who handles organizing and running the US Navy.

World War I—a war fought in Europe from 1914 to 1918.

World War II—a war fought in Europe, Asia, and Africa from 1939 to 1945.

★ WEBSITES ★

To learn more about the US Presidents, visit **booklinks.abdopublishing.com**. These links are routinely monitored and updated to provide the most current information available.

39

Index